PLANTS
on the Trail with
LEWIS AND CLARK

DOROTHY HINSHAW PATENT

Photographs by WILLIAM MUÑOZ

CLARION BOOKS · NEW YORK

Clarion Books
a Houghton Mifflin Company imprint
215 Park Avenue South, New York, NY 10003
Text copyright © 2003 by Dorothy Hinshaw Patent
Photographs copyright © 2003 by William Muñoz

The text was set in 15-point Breughel.
Map on pages vi–vii by Kayley LeFaiver

www.houghtonmifflinbooks.com

Manufactured in China

Library of Congress Cataloging-in-Publication Data

Patent, Dorothy Hinshaw.
Plants on the trail with Lewis and Clark / by Dorothy Hinshaw Patent ;
photos by William Muñoz.
p. cm.
Summary: Describes the journey of Lewis and Clark through the western
United States, focusing on the plants they cataloged, their uses for
food and medicine, and the plant lore of Native American people.
ISBN 0-618-06776-0 (alk. paper)
1. Lewis and Clark Expedition (1804-1806)–Juvenile literature. 2. Botany–West (U.S.)–
History–19th century–Juvenile literature. 3. Plant collecting–West (U.S.)–History–
19th century–Juvenile literature. 4. West (U.S.)–Description and travel–Juvenile literature.
5. Natural history–West (U.S.)–History–19th century–Juvenile literature. [1. Lewis and
Clark Expedition (1804-1806) 2. Botany–West (U.S.) 3. Natural history–West (U.S.)
4. West (U.S.)–Description and travel.] I. Muñoz, William, ill. II. Title.
F592.7 .P376 2003
581.978–dc21
2002010383

SCP 10 9 8 7 6 5 4 3 2 1

To all those who work to preserve the historical places of the western United States

Thanks to H. Wayne Phillips for help with the manuscript and the photos, and to Joseph Mussulman for help in answering questions about the expedition.

Contents

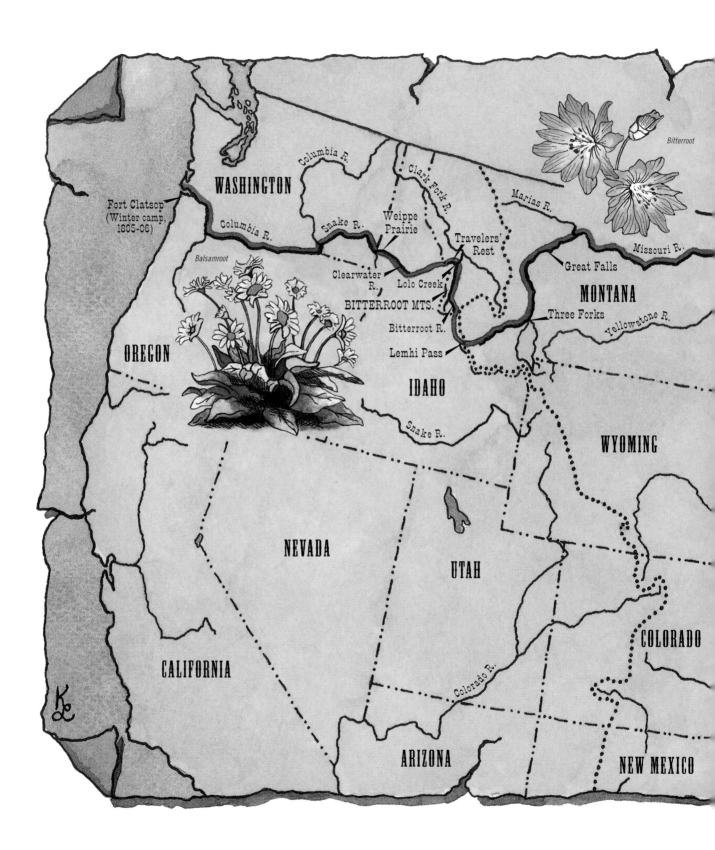

WASHINGTON

Columbia R.

Clark Fork R.

Marias R.

Bitterroot

Fort Clatsop
(Winter camp,
1805-06)

Columbia R.

Snake R.

Weippe
Prairie

Travelers'
Rest

Missouri R.

Great Falls

Balsamroot

Clearwater
R.

Lolo Creek

MONTANA

BITTERROOT MTS.

Three Forks

Yellowstone R.

OREGON

Bitterroot R.

Lemhi Pass

IDAHO

Snake R.

WYOMING

NEVADA

UTAH

CALIFORNIA

COLORADO

Colorado R.

ARIZONA

NEW MEXICO

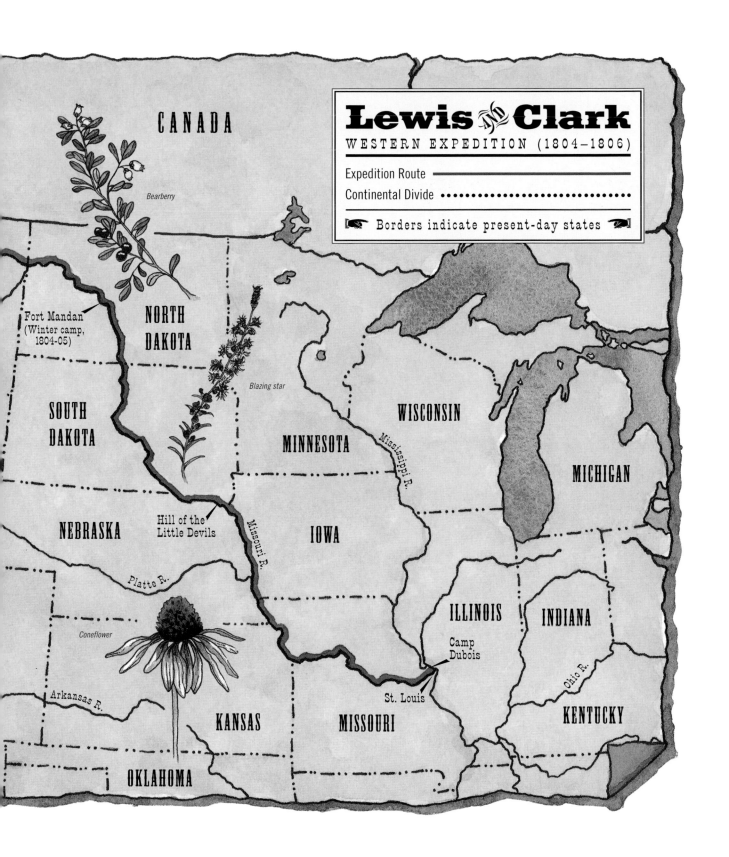

CANADA

Bearberry

Lewis and Clark
WESTERN EXPEDITION (1804–1806)

Expedition Route ————————
Continental Divide •••••••••••••••••••

Borders indicate present-day states

Fort Mandan
(Winter camp,
1804-05)

NORTH
DAKOTA

Blazing star

WISCONSIN

SOUTH
DAKOTA

MINNESOTA

MICHIGAN

Mississippi R.

NEBRASKA

Hill of the
Little Devils

IOWA

Missouri R.

Platte R.

ILLINOIS

INDIANA

Coneflower

Camp
Dubois

Ohio R.

Arkansas R.

KANSAS

St. Louis

MISSOURI

KENTUCKY

OKLAHOMA

Introduction

Thomas Jefferson became president in 1801, when the United States of America was a young country. The Constitution was only fourteen years old, and the country consisted of just sixteen states, all east of the Mississippi River. Jefferson, however, was already looking west, where he believed the nation's destiny lay.

Jefferson decided to send an army expedition westward to explore North America all the way from the Mississippi River to the Pacific Ocean, a distance of more than two thousand miles. By the time the expedition left in spring 1804, the

President Thomas Jefferson sent an expedition off to follow the Missouri River to its source and continue westward.

Louisiana Territory, which stretched from the western shore of the Mississippi River to the peaks of the Rocky Mountains, had just been purchased from the French. The land on the other side of the northern Rockies was up for grabs, with England, France, Russia, and Spain all interested in it. Spanish explorers in search of gold had penetrated the region, and a few fur trappers and traders worked along the lower part of the Missouri River and the faraway Pacific Coast. But otherwise, European Americans knew almost nothing about this vast landscape. The only spots located accurately on maps were the Mandan Indian villages along the Missouri River, in present-day North Dakota, and the mouth of the Columbia River, at the border between modern Washington and Oregon.

The expedition, which became known as the Corps of Discovery, traveled up the Missouri River from its mouth, where it enters the Mississippi River, to its source in the Rocky Mountains. After crossing the mountains, the expedition trav-

When the explorers began their long journey, they had no idea that the Rocky Mountains were as tall and rugged as they are. Here, balsamroot, a plant Lewis collected, blooms in sight of the Rockies.

Once they crossed the Rockies, the Corps of Discovery traveled down the Clearwater and Snake Rivers to reach the mighty Columbia.

eled to the Columbia River and followed it to the shores of the Pacific Ocean.

Jefferson chose his personal secretary, army captain Meriwether Lewis, as the leader of this difficult mission. He instructed Lewis to undertake an impressive list of goals: Find a water route across North America, meet with Indian tribes and discuss peaceful trade with them, map and describe this unknown region, and investigate the plant and animal life encountered along the way.

Lewis chose a man he had met earlier in the army, William Clark, to join him in command of the Corps of Discovery. Lewis and Clark complemented each other. Lewis knew more about science, but Clark was more knowledgeable about navigating a waterway like the Missouri, and he also was better at surveying the land.

Lewis wanted to leave in 1803, but getting ready took longer than expected, and the Corps of Discovery spent the winter of 1803-1804 camped by the Mississippi River across

The departure of the Corps of Discovery was delayed, so the men spent the winter of 1803-1804 at a spot near here, by Wood River, in Illinois.

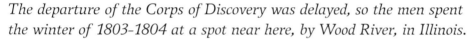

from St. Louis. The explorers, a group of approximately forty men, left in May 1804 and worked their way up the Missouri River through the prairies to the Mandan Indian villages, where they spent the winter of 1804–1805. They traveled in a 55-foot-long keelboat and two large rowboats called pirogues.

In April 1805, Lewis sent some of the men back to St. Louis in the keelboat with specimens, maps, letters, and journals. The expedition proceeded up the Missouri River in the pirogues and six canoes. In June, they reached the Great Falls of the Missouri River and had to transport everything overland around the waterfalls—except for one pirogue and some

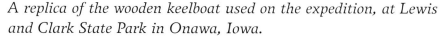

A replica of the wooden keelboat used on the expedition, at Lewis and Clark State Park in Onawa, Iowa.

They got to the Pacific Ocean in November 1805, just in time for winter.

of their gear, which they left behind. A month later, they put their boats back into the Missouri and continued westward.

In August 1805, they found the Shoshone Indians and traded for horses, which they needed to cross the Rocky Mountains. Getting through the rugged mountains was very difficult, but finally, in late September, they encountered the Nez Perce Indians on the western side of the Bitterroot Mountains. They left their horses with the Nez Perce and traveled by canoe down the Clearwater River to the Snake River, which led into the Columbia River.

They followed the wild Columbia to its mouth at the Pacific Ocean and settled in for the winter of 1805–1806 on a small river near the coast, naming the home they built Fort Clatsop, after the local Indian tribe. After a miserable, rainy winter, they headed back up the Columbia River and eventually returned to St. Louis in September 1806.

Jefferson had commanded Lewis and Clark to keep journals of their journey, and he asked them to encourage their men to do so as well. The journals of Lewis, Clark, and several of their men give us many fascinating details of the voyage. (Spelling and grammar weren't standardized yet in the early nineteenth century, so the quotations from the journals that appear in this book have been edited to make them clear.) Without these journals, we would know very little about the trip. But with them, we have a window on what the explorers saw and did, as well as information on previously unfamiliar Indian tribes, animals, and plants they encountered in the West.

1

Jefferson, Lewis, and Plants

*W*hen President Thomas Jefferson appointed Meriwether Lewis to command the expedition to explore western North America, one of his primary interests was the plant life. If the United States was to occupy this vast new land, the people would need to learn about its plants and their uses.

Jefferson was a scientist at heart, eager to learn all he could about the world around him and interested in gathering scientific knowledge. He had a passion for plants. "There is not a sprig of grass that shoots uninteresting to me," he wrote. He had begun taking notes on plants when he was

This portrait of Meriwether Lewis was painted by Charles Willson Peale after the Corps of Discovery returned. INDEPENDENCE NATIONAL HISTORIC PARK

twenty-three years old, and he kept up his botanical observations throughout his life.

At Monticello, his Virginia estate, Jefferson experimented with growing plants, including ones from Europe that he thought would contribute to the American economy. He wondered about the plants that grew in the West. Were there potential crop plants that the Indians cultivated or that grew

Thomas Jefferson was very interested in plants and had large gardens at his home, Monticello, in Virginia.

wild? Might some western shrubs or flowers be pleasing additions to American gardens?

Meriwether Lewis also had a special interest in plants. His mother was an herbalist, a person who knew the medical properties of plants and used them for healing. She grew herbs in her garden and also understood how to use wild plants, and she taught her son what she knew. In those days, all medicines came from nature, not from the laboratory, and herbalists provided a vital medical service.

Lewis learned how to use healing plants from his mother and used chokecherry wood to help cure himself during the expedition.

Jefferson also taught Lewis about plants. The two men would stroll through Monticello's gardens, and Jefferson would point out special plants or explain the scientific system of giving each species of plant and animal two Latin names.

In March 1803, Jefferson sent Lewis to Philadelphia to strengthen his scientific background before beginning the western exploration. There Lewis studied with Benjamin Smith Barton, professor of botany at the University of Pennsylvania. Although there is no written record, Barton probably taught Lewis how to prepare botanical specimens. When plants are properly collected, pressed, and dried, they become vital scientific reference material. With Barton's help, Lewis learned the scientific terms to describe his finds. He also bought a copy of Barton's botany textbook, the first in the United States, to take along on the expedition.

Lewis was a born naturalist, a scientist who makes his observations directly from nature rather than in the laboratory. In Lewis's time, the study of nature as a science was just beginning. Few scientists studied their subjects in laboratories.

Lewis was so eager to learn about new plants that in March 1804, even before the expedition left the St. Louis area, he sent Jefferson cuttings from a tree now called the Osage orange. He got the cuttings from trees cultivated in St. Louis, but the originals grew in an Osage Indian village three hundred miles to the west. The tree was unknown east of the Mississippi. Lewis

Lewis began his plant collection while at Wood River. The Osage orange was the first plant he collected and described.

wrote to Jefferson, "The Indians give an extravagant account of the exquisite odor of this fruit." He described what he had learned about the structure of the fruit, which he hadn't seen for himself, since it was early springtime.

Lewis's greatest strength as a naturalist lay in his careful observation of animals and plants. He wrote extensively in his journals and gave detailed descriptions of many species of plants. In those descriptions, Lewis used at least two hundred different scientific terms correctly. For example, he described star-shaped structures as "stellate," and leaves with lobes resembling a hand with the fingers spread as "palmate."

Sometimes he would just make quick notes, but often he gave interesting tidbits of information, such as this description on April 14, 1805, of the landscape in what is now western North Dakota: "On these hills many aromatic herbs are seen; resembling in taste, smell, and appearance, the sage, hysop, wormwood, southernwood, and two other herbs which are strangers to me; the one resembling the camphor in taste and smell. . . . The other, about the same size, has a long, narrow, smooth soft leaf of an agreeable smell and flavor; of this last the antelope is very fond; they feed on it, and perfume the hair of their foreheads and necks with it by rubbing against it."

Lewis's wide knowledge of the plants that lived in eastern North America came in very handy during the journey. He

Lewis might have described the star-shaped flower of the salmonberry as "stellate."

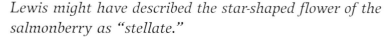

Lewis found that many plants familiar in the East, such as cattails, also live in the West.

extended the known range of many eastern plants, such as the box elder (or ash-leafed maple), which occurs along the Missouri River all the way to the base of the Rocky Mountains. He found that both cattails and the broad-leaved arrowhead, which were familiar eastern marsh plants, also lived along the faraway Pacific Coast. He often contrasted the plants he found with their eastern relatives. Lewis compared the wild Jerusalem artichokes that he found in April 1805 with the cultivated variety grown in American gardens: "The flavor of this root resembles that of the Jerusalem artichoke, and the stalk of the weed which produces it is also similar, though both the root and the stalk are much smaller than the Jerusalem artichoke."

As Lewis studied a plant, he used all his senses. He could put a lot of information into a few words. Here's what he wrote about a plant he found in the Bitterroot Mountains in June 1806: "There is an abundance of a species of angelica in

Lewis wrote a detailed description of this plant, now called licorice root or lovage. He thought it was a different plant, a kind of angelica.
H. WAYNE PHILLIPS

When Clark wrote about the tallgrass prairie, he could have been describing this scene.

these mountains much stronger to the taste and more highly scented than that species common to the U. States. Know of no particular virtue or property it possesses; the natives dry it and cut it in small pieces which they string on a small cord and place about their necks; it smells very pleasantly." In just a few words we learn that this plant is aromatic, abundant, and strongly flavored, and though not useful in a practical way, was gathered by the Indians for its enjoyable properties.

As the expedition progressed, Lewis noticed changes in vegetation. Below the Great Falls of the Missouri River, he saw his first narrowleaf cottonwood tree. He realized that above the falls it was replacing plains cottonwood. The next day, as the Corps of Discovery entered the Rocky Mountains, he commented, "There is not any of the broad leafed [plains] cottonwood on the river since it has entered the mountains." He also noted which habitat the various plants preferred, such as moist, shaded soil or a dry, sunny slope.

Journals by Lewis covering long periods of time are missing. For example, from May 20, 1804, to April 7, 1805, the only known journal entries by him are for September 16 and 17, 1804, found on pages torn from one of the typical red

Eastern cottonwoods, like this one along the Yellowstone River, become less and less common the farther west one travels.

notebooks used for the journals. He did, however, make some separate scientific notes. No one knows if he didn't write in the usual journals during this time and during other gaps or if some journals were lost.

Fortunately for us, William Clark also took note of the plants. Here's an example of Clark's writing, describing the tallgrass prairie and nearby environment in Kansas on July 4, 1804: "The plains of this country are covered with a leek-green grass, well calculated for the sweetest and most nourishing hay—interspersed with copses [thickets] of trees, spreading their lofty branches over pools, springs, or brooks of fine water. Groups of shrubs covered with the most delicious fruit are to be seen in every direction, and nature appears to have exerted herself to beautify the scenery by the variety of flowers."

Whenever he could, Lewis collected and dried specimens as he had been taught in Philadelphia. His preserved specimens often had only a simple label identifying where he had collected it and when. Unfortunately, many of his specimens were lost. When the Corps of Discovery encountered the Great Falls of the Missouri, Lewis hid the plants he had collected since leaving the Mandan villages, along with one of the pirogues, in a protected place called a cache. Spring floods in 1806 destroyed every single one, as Lewis discovered on the return trip in July of that year. We will never know how many species he collected and lost, since no list of these specimens has ever been found.

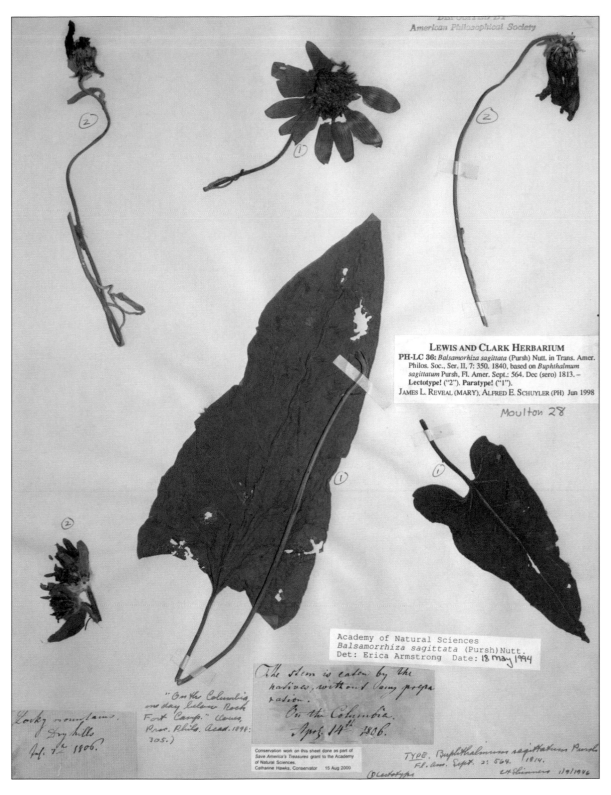

LEWIS AND CLARK HERBARIUM
PH-LC 36: *Balsamorhiza sagittata* (Pursh) Nutt. in Trans. Amer.
Philos. Soc., Ser. II, 7: 350. 1840, based on *Buphthalmum
sagittatum* Pursh, Fl. Amer. Sept.: 564. Dec (sero) 1813. –
Lectotype! ("2"). Paratype! ("1").
JAMES L. REVEAL (MARY), ALFRED E. SCHUYLER (PH) Jun 1998

Moulton 28

Academy of Natural Sciences
Balsamorrhiza sagittata (Pursh)Nutt.
Det: Erica Armstrong   Date: 18 May 1994

*The stem is eaten by the
natives, without any prepa-
ration.
On the Columbia.
April 14th 1806.*

*Rocky mountains.
Dry hills
Jul. 7th 1806.*

*"On the Columbia
one day below Rock
Fort Camp." Coues,
Proc. Phila. Acad.1898:
305.)*

Conservation work on this sheet done as part of
Save America's Treasures grant to the Academy
of Natural Sciences.
Catharine Hawks, Conservator   15 Aug 2000

TYPE. *Buphthalmum sagittatum* Pursh
Fl. Am. Sept. 2: 564. 1814.
(!) Lectotype   E.A. Simmers 11/9/1946

Lewis collected these specimens of arrowleaf balsamroot on April 14 and
July 7, 1806. To preserve them properly, he had to tend to them even
while traveling. LEWIS AND CLARK HERBARIUM, AMERICAN PHILOSOPHICAL SOCIETY.
PHOTO COURTESY OF THE ACADEMY OF NATURAL SCIENCES, PHILADELPHIA.

Yarrow is one of the plants Lewis collected while staying with the Nez Perce in the spring of 1806.

The quality of Lewis's surviving plant specimens is amazing, considering their age and the difficult conditions on the trail. Preparing and preserving plants is a time-consuming and demanding process. A specimen has to be spread out properly, then pressed between two sheets of blotting paper. The paper soaks up the moisture from the specimen, drying it out. The specimen must be removed, aired, and placed between fresh sheets until it is completely dry, so it won't rot. There were times when Lewis had to deal with a large number of plants all at once. While he stayed with the Nez Perce Indians, for example, he had between thirty and fifty specimens to tend to every day. While handling them and moving them about, he had to be sure to keep the identification tags with the correct specimens. All this had to be accomplished under rough conditions, with no tables to work on.

How did Lewis decide which plants to describe and/or preserve? Plants in flower were obvious to the eye and were often noted and collected. But Lewis was always on the lookout for useful plants—plants that might do well in gardens or

It is hard to miss striking flowers like pink elephants when they are in bloom.

The golden currant, named for the color of its flowers, can have yellow, red, or black fruit. It is one of the species Lewis brought back, hoping it would become popular.

might serve as medicines. After tasting one kind of wild currant, he wrote that it "would be preferred at our markets to any currant now cultivated in the U. States." He brought back seeds of this fruit, as well as many of the others he found, for Jefferson to plant in his garden.

Of a dwarf juniper he saw on the open prairie, he wrote that it "seldom ever rises more than six inches high . . . they would make a handsome edging to the borders of a garden." Today a variety of this species is often used as a ground cover in yards.

Lewis was a great observer and collector, but what he described or gathered depended on the season when he passed through a particular area. He noticed and collected wildflowers in bloom and probably didn't notice other, equally interesting, species that were not flowering at the time.

When the Corps of Discovery was on the move, collecting was more difficult. It is not surprising that more plants were collected at Camp Chopunnish, near present-day Kamiah, Idaho, than at any other location; the explorers stayed there

Stretches of the Bitterroot River of western Montana look much the same as they did two hundred years ago.

for more than three weeks in 1806, waiting for the snow to melt in the Bitterroot Mountains. But even when the expedition traveled quickly, Lewis wrote general descriptions of the plant life in his journals, whether or not he had the opportunity to collect specimens. While passing through the prairies in April 1805, he wrote that the landscape was "one continued level fertile plain as far as the eye can reach, in which there is not even a solitary tree or shrub to be seen." He added that the land was covered by "a short grass resembling very much the bluegrass." This was probably western bluegrass.

As the Corps of Discovery traveled up the Bitterroot River in what is now Montana in September 1805, Lewis wrote, "The valley of this river is generally a prairie and from five to six miles wide. The growth is almost altogether pine, principally of the long-leafed kind, with some spruce and a kind of fir resembling the Scotch fir. Near the watercourses we find a small proportion of the narrow-leafed cottonwood, some redwood honeysuckle, and rose bushes [that] form a scant proportion of the underbrush to be seen." Lewis paints a vivid picture that we can see in our mind's eye.

Plants, however, were much more than scientific specimens to the Corps of Discovery. They also served as building material, food, and medicine. Without the help of the plants they found along the way, the explorers would never have been able to complete their journey.

2

The Importance of Trees

*T*rees were especially important to the success of the Lewis and Clark expedition. In the early 1800s, wood was the chief material for construction. The keelboat and pirogues that took the expedition upriver were made of wood, as were the paddles and poles the men used to power them. When a paddle or pole broke, the explorers had to make a new one from wood found along their route.

Not long after departing from the St. Louis area, the Corps of Discovery left the woodlands and entered the prairie. Few trees grow in prairies except near the rivers and streams,

Cottonwood trees provided welcome shade and protection from wind and rain.

where there is enough water for them to survive. The explorers came to value the trees along the river, which gave them protection from downpours and welcome shade when they stopped for meals.

Wood was also important as fuel. The Corps of Discovery was divided into three messes, or groups, each of which ate separately. Each mess needed a fire to cook the evening meal, so wood gathering for fuel was a daily activity.

Cottonwoods were the tallest trees along the Missouri River, sometimes reaching more than a hundred feet in height. Often they were the only trees. Cottonwood trees grow quickly and have soft wood, which splits under stress and isn't very good for building things. But by the time the Corps of Discovery reached the Mandan and Hidatsa Indian villages, cottonwood was the only wood available in sufficient abundance for construction of their winter home. Fortunately, the men were able

A replica of Fort Mandan has been built near the original location.
The original was constructed mostly of cottonwood.

to find enough tall, straight trees, and they ended up building a sturdy fort, which they named Fort Mandan. During that very cold winter, cottonwood burning in big fireplaces kept the men warm and cooked their meals.

The explorers spent lots of time with the Indians during the winter. Together they hunted for buffalo and other game, and the Indians told of the tribes and landscapes to the west. Lewis was always interested in how the Native Americans used plants, and he was surprised to learn that the Mandan collected cottonwood branches to feed their horses—the animals would eat the bark.

At Fort Mandan, Lewis and Clark hired a French Canadian trapper named Toussaint Charbonneau as an interpreter. He had two teenage wives, who were Shoshone Indians. When the Corps of Discovery left Fort Mandan in April 1805 to continue their westward journey, Charbonneau brought along only one wife, Sacagawea, and their infant son, Jean Baptiste, born in February 1805. Lewis and Clark had learned from the Indians that the Rocky Mountains were tall and rugged, and they knew that they would have to get horses from the Shoshone to cross the mountains. Having someone along who spoke their language was vital.

Sacagawea's name has been spelled more than a dozen different ways. Most white scholars of Lewis and Clark today spell the name "Sacagawea." This spelling is based on the

Few trees grow in the prairies, which once almost completely covered the middle third of North America.

Mandan version of her name, which means "Bird Woman." The Lemhi Shoshone Indians, who are descendents of her tribe, prefer the spelling "Sacajawea," which means "One Who Carries a Burden" in their language.

As the expedition traveled westward up the Missouri River that spring, the land got drier and drier. Fewer and fewer trees grew along the river. The Indians had told Lewis and Clark of a great waterfall, but they said the expedition could get around it in a day or two.

Lewis was traveling on land ahead of the boats when he confronted the Great Falls of the Missouri River on June 13, 1805. Awestruck, he wrote, "Projecting rocks below receive the water in its passage down and break it into a perfect white foam which assumes a thousand forms in a moment, sometimes flying up in jets of sparkling foam to the height of fifteen or twenty feet. . . ."

As Lewis continued along the shore, he realized that the Indians had been mistaken. The falls punctuated the river for more than sixteen miles, and the Corps of Discovery would have to portage, or carry their gear overland, around the falls.

Lewis and Clark wondered how they would manage to move all their gear using only manpower. They decided to build wagons and sent one of the men, Sergeant Patrick Gass, to look for trees. He found a lone, large cottonwood tree, almost two feet in diameter. Lewis believed it was the only big tree within twenty miles.

The men cut it down, then sawed the trunk crosswise into rounds, which became wagon wheels. The cottonwood also worked for making the bodies of two rough wagons and for the various other parts necessary to construct them. The axles, which would take great stress as they rolled over the prairie, were made from the hardwood mast of the pirogue they planned to cache.

The expedition finally got under way again on July 15, 1805.

Luckily, a single large cottonwood, perhaps like this one, grew near the Great Falls.

Soon the landscape changed. First, rocky cliffs bordered by hills hugged the riverbanks. The buffalo disappeared, making it harder to find meat. The expedition was approaching the Rocky Mountains, where the forests of abundant pine, fir, and other evergreen trees would present a new challenge.

The men spent weeks looking for the Shoshone Indians and finally made contact in mid-August 1805. The Shoshone had never seen white men and at first feared that the

The landscape around Lemhi Pass, where the Corps of Discovery found the Shoshone Indians, hasn't changed much in two hundred years. The waters of this little creek flow eastward and eventually become the great Missouri River.

strangers might be dangerous. Luckily, the chief turned out to be Sacagawea's brother, which dispelled any distrust the Indians felt toward these strange-looking people.

The Shoshone traded some of their horses for the white men's goods. To make wooden pack saddles, the men cut off the blades of their oars and took apart boxes that held some of their gear. The gear was then transferred into rawhide bags. In this way they were able to make twenty saddles, which were enough to carry the items they decided to take along over the mountains. Anything that wasn't necessary was carefully cached, to be picked up on the way back.

In September 1805 the Corps of Discovery left the Shoshone and began its struggle through the Rocky Mountains. The most difficult time came in the Bitterroot Mountains, where they endured snow and sleet as their horses stumbled through the dense forests, tripping over downed wood on the forest floor. Despite the hardships, Lewis took the time to note new trees they encountered, such as those now called whitebark pine, Englemann spruce, subalpine fir, and more.

Once they got through the Rockies, they had to make new canoes to travel down rivers to the Pacific Coast. The Nez Perce Indians, who fed the almost starving explorers on the Pacific side of the mountains, showed the men how to make canoes by burning out the centers of logs instead of chopping them out with axes. This proved to be a much easier way of

*The lodgepole pine was one of the trees Lewis observed as
the expedition struggled through the Rocky Mountains.*

constructing canoes. They used five ponderosa pines, another
species new to science.

Leaving their horses with the Nez Perce for the winter and
caching the pack saddles, the explorers launched their canoes
into the Clearwater River in early October and sped toward

the Columbia. It was rough going, through deep gorges with white-water rapids, but the simple ponderosa dugouts worked surprisingly well. By the time they reached the Snake River near what is now the Idaho-Washington border, the forests were gone and grassland had reappeared.

On October 16, 1805, the Corps of Discovery reached the great Columbia River. The banks of the river held many Indian

The men made dugout canoes like this one to travel down the Clearwater and Snake Rivers and then down the Columbia.

The dugouts were made from large ponderosa pines.

villages, where people gathered to dry the abundant harvest of salmon. The Indians all lived along the river, for this was a land of little rainfall, and trees grew only near rivers and streams. The Indians used the wood to build racks for drying the salmon.

After successfully navigating and sometimes portaging around the many rapids of the upper Columbia, the expedition reached the passage of the river through the Cascade Moun-

The Indians of the Columbia River area dried salmon on wooden racks similar to those in this photo taken near Port Angeles, Washington, in the early 1900s.
NORTH OLYMPIC LIBRARY

tains. In a few miles, the landscape changed completely. Dry grass prairies were replaced by heavily forested hills and mountains, and gray skies supplanted blue ones. West of the mountains, abundant rain fell, nourishing vast forests of huge trees.

The towering ancient Pacific forests amazed the men. Clark wrote of the Sitka spruce near the mouth of the Columbia River: They "grow here to an immense size and height, many of them 7 and 8 feet through and upwards of 200 feet high."

The Pacific coastal forest is cool and moist, providing a perfect home for many kinds of plants.

After exploring the area and enduring violent rainstorms, the men decided to settle for the winter on the banks of a small river near the south side of the Columbia. Finding wood to build the fort was no problem. As Sergeant Gass wrote, "We have found a kind of timber in plenty which splits freely and makes the finest puncheons [planks] I have ever seen." We aren't sure today which kind of tree Gass was talking about, but it was probably spruce. Because it split so well, the spruce would have been used for making the doors, floors, and roof. Other kinds of wood probably went into making the fort, too. Hemlock was the most abundant tree, and its slim, straight trunks would have been perfect for constructing the walls, which were almost certainly made of small logs.

Eager to get protection from the miserable rainy weather, the men hurried to build their winter home. They named it Fort Clatsop, after the major local Indian tribe. They also used wood to make beds, tables, benches, and stools.

A replica of Fort Clatsop stands close to the original site. In a room like this, Lewis spent hours writing descriptions of the animals and plants the explorers had encountered.

The majestic Sitka spruce is one of the trees Lewis described at Fort Clatsop.

In this place they spent the gloomy winter of 1805–1806. Rain fell almost constantly, and the sun rarely peeked through the clouds. Protected from the elements by the solid wood logs of the fort, Lewis spent hour after hour at his desk writing descriptions of the plants and animals found along the route, including such different plants as the deer fern, Oregon grape, and Sitka spruce.

During the winter, Lewis learned how important trees were to the Chinookan tribes of the lower Columbia region,

Lewis collected the deer fern while at Fort Clatsop.

This lone western redcedar in Tofino, British Columbia, is about eight hundred years old. When Lewis and Clark reached the Pacific Coast, they encountered forests with many giants like this one.

Western redcedar was an especially important tree to the Indians of the coast.

especially western redcedar. The Indians made thread from its bark and used both pine and cedar to make bowls, platters, and spoons. They cut down several kinds of trees to build their lodges, and made cords out of cedar bark to lash posts and rafters together. Cedar is especially durable, so they built their roofs from it. Because such huge trees grew in the coastal forests, the dugouts of the Chinookan tribes could be large. Some of these boats were fifty feet long and carried up to thirty passengers.

3

Plants as Food

$\mathcal{L}$ewis and Clark expected to be able to hunt and gather food as they traveled. They knew, however, that they couldn't count on nature alone, so they brought along simple, if monotonous, basic provisions. When no wild food was available, the cooks served up meals using lard and hominy (a form of corn) one day, flour and salt pork the next, and pork and cornmeal the third day. Then the cycle began again.

Game provided the main source of wild food. Big animals like buffalo, deer, and elk provided the large quantities needed to fuel the strenuous paddling and poling of the boats against

As they traveled, the men of the Corps of Discovery ate mostly game, such as the abundant buffalo.

the strong Missouri River current. The men ate huge amounts of meat—up to nine pounds each daily when they could get it!

A heavy meat diet, however, is not healthy. By June 1804, the men were becoming ill with skin problems, such as painful boils. Drinking the scummy river water and eating spoiled meat were probably partly to blame, but the limited diet also deprived the men of important vitamins and other nutrients. Tender skin and wounds that don't heal are symptoms of scurvy (a disease caused by a lack of vitamin C), and some historians believe that the Corps of Discovery suffered off and on from this disorder.

The explorers did include some wild plants in their diet, however. Lewis noted in late May 1804 that his men made use of a kind of cress that grows along the shores of the Missouri and found it "a very pleasant wholesome salad." They also gathered what they called wild kale along the river and boiled it.

By mid-July, the prairie began showing its abundance. Clark wrote in his journal, "I saw great quantities of grapes, plums of 2 kinds, wild cherries of 2 kinds, hazelnuts, and gooseberries." But collecting wild foods was time-consuming. Finding enough fruit and vegetables for the forty or so men was usually impractical.

Special occasions, however, provided a reason for spending time harvesting these foods. For his thirty-fourth birthday on August 1, 1804, Clark wrote, "I ordered a saddle of fat venison, an elk fleece, and a beavertail to be cooked and a dessert of cherries, plums, raspberries, currants, and grapes of a superior quality." Beavertail was a rich, fatty delicacy. An elk fleece must have meant a special cut of meat, such as the loin.

The travelers learned from the Native Americans about local foods. The Plains Indians harvested many wild foods, including the root of a small plant called the white apple, breadroot, or prairie turnip. This was important in the diet of many Plains Indian tribes. Lewis wrote, "The white apple appears to me to be a tasteless, insipid food of itself, though I

*The starchy root of the prairie turnip was eaten raw or cooked in
a number of different ways.* H. WAYNE PHILLIPS

have no doubt but it is a very healthy and moderately nutritious food." The Indians generally combined it with meat, buffalo fat, and/or berries.

Plains Indians living along the Missouri River, such as the Arikara, Mandan, and Hidatsa, grew garden vegetables, especially beans, corn, and squash. The Corps of Discovery received these important foods as gifts and also traded for them.

During the winter of 1804–1805, these crops, especially corn, became vital to the survival of the explorers. They learned to eat many Indian foods, including a favorite treat

Chokecherries were an ingredient in a stew the Indians cooked.

consisting of boiled squash, beans, corn, and wild choke-cherries. In order to get corn from the Mandan and Hidatsa, one of the men, blacksmith John Shields, set up a metal forge. He repaired the Indians' weapons and cooking pots in trade for this food. Later on, he manufactured battle axes and traded pieces of metal. Without corn from the Mandan, it is doubtful that the Corps of Discovery would have survived that winter.

The Corps of Discovery left Fort Mandan on April 7, 1805. On April 9, Sacagawea was already finding food. She knew which greens and roots could be eaten and where to find the different kinds of wild foods. As soon as the expedition stopped for dinner that night, she dug up roots of wild Jerusalem artichokes. While the journals contain only a few mentions of Sacagawea's food-gathering efforts, she almost certainly contributed fresh fruit and vegetables to the explorers' diet on a regular basis.

While with the Shoshone, Lewis and Clark noted some of the plants the Indians ate. They mixed sunflower seeds and

Sacagawea gathered the roots of wild Jerusalem artichokes like these to nourish the explorers.

The Shoshone gathered serviceberries to use in a kind of bread.

those of a relative of spinach called lamb's quarters with serviceberries and pounded them into a sort of bread. Lewis also tasted some of the roots eaten by the Shoshone. He described one as "agreeably flavored," and said of another, a kind of sunflower, that it was "certainly the best root I have yet seen in use among the Indians." Of the bitterroot, which was very popular with many tribes, Lewis wrote: "They became perfectly soft by boiling, but had a very bitter taste, which was nauseous to my palate, and I transferred them to the Indians, who ate them heartily."

When the Corps of Discovery stumbled out of the Bitterroot Mountains onto Weippe Prairie in September 1805, the

Nez Perce Indians rescued them from starvation by feeding them bulbs of blue camas. Camas blooms in the spring with beautiful blue flowers, so the explorers didn't see the plants in bloom then. On the return trip in June 1806, camas in bloom delighted Clark, who wrote: "At a short distance it resembles a lake of fine clear water. So complete is this deception that on first sight I could have sworn it was water."

The camas has beautiful blue flowers.

Camas stores energy in the bulbs, which the Indians collected for food.

During the summer, the camas plant stores energy for the next year's growth in a fat underground bulb. Camas bulbs formed a very important part of the diet for the Indians, who regularly gathered them in the fall. Clark described in detail how the Nez Perce cooked the bulbs in pits and either dried them or made them into a form of bread. In either form, the camas kept well for a long time and helped feed the Indians during the winter.

Tribes along the Columbia River and Pacific Coast also relied on roots and bulbs of plants for a major part of their diet. While at Fort Clatsop during the winter of 1805-1806, Lewis had the opportunity to learn about many of the plants that the Indians enjoyed eating and to try some of them for himself. Coastal Indians ate roots of the edible thistle, horsetail, western bracken fern, and cattail. Of the bracken fern root, Lewis wrote that, once roasted, it was "much like wheat dough and not very unlike it in flavor, though it has also a pungency which becomes more visible after you have chewed it for some time; this pungency was disagreeable to me, but the natives eat it voraciously and I have no doubt but it is a very nutritious food."

These Indians also relished the bulb of the broad-leaved arrowhead, which they called wapato. In order to collect the bulbs, the women would travel by canoe to the swampy areas

The bulbs of the wapato were a very important food for the Indians living along the lower Columbia River area.

Huckleberries are one of the most delicious wild fruits in America.

where wapato grew. Then they would get into the water and use their feet to loosen the bulbs from the mud. They sometimes waded so deeply to obtain this delicacy that the water came up to their necks. The loose bulbs, about the size of chicken eggs, floated to the top, where the women collected them. When roasted, wapato has a taste similar to potatoes. Wapato was a major trade item among the Indians. Lewis wrote, "The natives of the sea coast and lower part of the river will dispose of their most valuable articles to obtain this root."

Lewis collected many fine, previously unknown fruits and berries, including various currants and gooseberries. He described and collected one of the most distinctive fruits in North America in the Rocky Mountains, the mountain huckleberry. These deep purple berries are relatives of the garden blueberry, but their flavor is much more intense. Lewis also noted a close relative, the whortleberry, a small bush that grows at high elevations and bears small, delicious red fruit. Chances are that the expedition encountered a number of species of tasty huckleberries, since at least fifteen different kinds are found in the Rocky Mountains. A much larger species, which grows as tall as eight feet, lives in the Columbia River Valley and was also collected by Lewis. The Indians enjoyed eating the small purple berries.

The deep purple fruit of a bush called salal was another favorite among the coastal Indians. They baked it into large

The red huckleberry, which lives on the Pacific Coast, produces large bushes rather than the small ones of the species that live in the Rocky Mountains.

loaves. Clark wrote that at one camp an Indian woman fed him soup "made of bread of the *shele wele* [his word for salal] berries mixed with roots." More familiar fruits such as cranberries and crab apples also grew along the coast and were enjoyed by the natives. The Indians, according to Lewis, made loaves from huckleberries: "Very frequently they pound them and bake them in large loaves of ten to fifteen pounds; this bread keeps very well during one season and retains the moist juices of the fruit much better than any other method of preservation. This bread is broken and stirred in cold water until it be sufficiently thick and then eaten."

Other fruits noted by Lewis that were eaten by the Columbia River tribes include the thimbleberry. According to Lewis, the Indians ate the young shoots of this plant raw. He also collected the salmonberry, a pinkish fruit similar to a raspberry, and took note of the Pacific blackberry.

In May 1806, on the return trip through Idaho, Sacagawea busied herself collecting roots of the yampah, which have a licoricelike flavor. She gathered large quantities of these roots and dried them to help provide food on the difficult trip through the Bitterroot Mountains. Another root that she might have collected is called cous. Lewis and Clark spelled the word "cows." On May 10, 1806, Clark wrote of one Indian village: "The noise of their women pounding the cows roots reminds me of a nail factory."

Yampah was a useful food for the Shoshone, as they could dig the roots and store them to eat when food was scarce.
H. WAYNE PHILLIPS

In June 1806, Sacagawea collected roots of the western springbeauty, a relative of the bitterroot, in the Bitterroot Mountains. Clark tells us that Sacagawea collected the roots. Lewis merely writes that he "met with a plant the root of which the Shoshone eat."

The springbeauty is closely related to the bitterroot, and the Indians ate the roots of both. H. Wayne Phillips

After crossing the Bitterroots on the return trip, the expedition split up. Lewis and nine other men took a shortcut to the Great Falls, while Sacagawea accompanied Clark and the majority of the expedition back the way they had come, then down the Yellowstone River to the Missouri. According to Clark's journals, Sacagawea continued to collect and share food during this time.

4

Wildflowers and Their Uses

As the Corps of Discovery worked its way west, Lewis noted many beautiful wildflowers. Wildflowers are at their glory when they burst into bloom, most often in the spring and early summer. Lewis collected sixty plant specimens, many of them wildflowers, along the lower Missouri River on the expedition's way to the Mandan villages in 1804. He sent them back to St. Louis on the keelboat from the Mandan villages in April 1805. Unfortunately, more than thirty mysteriously disappeared. Some of these were prairie wildflowers. The prairie was again in bloom in the spring of 1805, and Lewis continued to collect.

Lewis may have collected the rough blazing star, along with many other beautiful prairie wildflowers that didn't survive to be included in the Lewis and Clark Herbarium.

But all of these specimens were destroyed when the cache at the Great Falls was flooded.

Lewis collected few plants of any kind during the dreary winter of 1805–1806 at Fort Clatsop. He gathered a few wildflowers as the explorers worked their way back up the Columbia River in the spring of 1806. When the Corps of Discovery once again reached Nez Perce territory in what is now Idaho, Lewis had an opportunity to sample the abundant variety of spring blossoms that he had noticed when deep snow stalled the expedition on the west side of the Bitterroot Mountains:

bright yellow rough wallflower, pretty pink showy phlox, rich purple Douglas's clematis, blue silky lupine, and others.

Although Lewis wrote scientifically accurate descriptions of many plants and preserved specimens of them correctly, he never gave them the Latin names that scientists use for precise identification. If he had, he would have gotten credit for recording the first scientific descriptions of many of the plants he collected. Since he didn't, that honor had to wait until botanist Frederick Pursh named many of his specimens a few years after the expedition had returned.

Pursh chose to honor William Clark in naming a pretty pink flower that Lewis collected and described while with the Nez Perce in 1806. One common name for this lovely flower is ragged robin. The petals are so deeply lobed that they look as if

Clarkia, *also called ragged robin, has deeply lobed, bright pink petals.*

they have been torn, giving it its common name. Pursh gave it the scientific name *Clarkia pulchella*. *Pulchella* means "beautiful." A hillside cloaked by these intense pink blossoms gleams in the sunlight.

One of the most interesting plants Lewis documented is the bitterroot, now the state flower of Montana. Bitterroot grows in dry, gravelly soil in open areas. It sends up its modest dark green leaves soon after snowmelt. The leaves gather the sun's energy and send nutrients to its roots, then wither. When the ground warms in June, the roots send up buds that open into large, delicate pink flowers. After the flowers wither, only the roots remain to survive the heat and drought of summer.

When the bitterroot blooms, only the flowers appear above the ground.

Some western Indian tribes still dig bitterroots for food.

Pursh gave the bitterroot its scientific name, *Lewisia redi-*
viva, after Meriwether Lewis. The very appropriate name *redi-*
viva means "comes back to life." Even after being completely
dried out for a year or more, bitterroots can sprout and grow
without being watered. In 1862, to keep them from growing, a
British scientist boiled the roots he'd been sent—but they still
showed signs of life and "produced beautiful flowers in great
perfection" two years after being collected.

When the leaves of the bitterroot become visible, the Indians
use specially designed pointed sticks to dig up the roots, which
are fleshy and tender at this time. They peel off the tough outer

covering, then boil or bake the white core. The bitter taste fades when the roots are cooked. Bitterroot can also be dried to form a meal, like cornmeal, that can be stored for later use.

Lewis first collected the bitterroot on July 1, 1806, near one of the expedition's most important campsites, Travelers' Rest. The Corps of Discovery stopped at this site before crossing the Bitterroot Mountains in 1805, and once again on the return trip in 1806. It was here that Lewis and Clark split up for their two separate routes back to the Missouri River.

Bear grass grows over a wide range in the West. The Indians made baskets and clothing from its tough, thin leaves.

The Clatsop Indians made hats like this, using redcedar bark and bear grass leaves.

Wildflowers can be useful as well as beautiful. While at Fort Clatsop, Lewis wrote about how the Indians along the Pacific Coast used bear grass, also called Indian basket grass. They combined it with redcedar bark to weave watertight cooking baskets and waterproof hats.

Throughout human history, people have recognized that some plants have medicinal properties. Today "medicine" means pills and injections, but before laboratories began developing chemicals for treating diseases, most medicines came from plants.

On the keelboat that was sent back to St. Louis in 1805, Lewis included samples of a coneflower as an example of a plant the Indians used as medicine.

Jefferson instructed Lewis to learn what remedies the Indians had, and Lewis commented in his journals on how they used some plants as treatments. One especially interesting example is the purple coneflower, which grows in the prairie. The Indians gathered its roots to treat a number of poisonous conditions, such as snakebite and bee stings, as well as toothaches. Lewis sent a specimen to Jefferson from Fort Mandan.

A chief of the Arikara Indians, who accompanied the expedition to the Mandan villages, gave Lewis information about a number of healing plants. The seeds of a particular honeysuckle could be used to make a diuretic tea. Another prairie flower produced leaves that could be crushed in a little water to make eyedrops.

Lewis gathered many of his specimens while traveling, not while staying with Indians, so he wasn't able to learn how much Native Americans relied on them to treat medical conditions. We know from other sources, for example, that they used the lovely blanket flower, which is common on western grasslands, in many ways: to treat intestinal infections, skin problems, and kidney disorders. It also came in handy for making nose drops and eyewash.

The Indians found medicinal uses for a great many plants, including the blanket flower.

Lewis treated an infection of one of his men with wild ginger.
H. Wayne Phillips

When his men needed medical attention, Lewis sometimes used natural remedies instead of relying on the limited medical chest he had brought along. On June 18, 1806, one of the men, John Potts, cut his leg badly with a knife. Lewis was able to stem the bleeding, but the wound became infected and painful, so on June 22, Lewis applied some cous roots to the wound, which seemed to help. On June 27, the wound was better, but it still hadn't healed. Lewis found some wild ginger growing in the forest of the Bitterroot Mountains. He wrote, "We applied the pounded roots and leaves of the wild ginger and from which he found great relief."

Today, some of the plants Lewis collected are still a part of modern treatments. Wild ginger helps against fever, colds, and indigestion, as well as being used for healing wounds. The purple coneflower helps stimulate the immune system, making it easier for people to fight off infections. Herbalists today use many other native plants as well.

5

The Fate of Lewis's Specimens

After the keelboat carrying Lewis's collection of plants and other scientific specimens from the lower Missouri River arrived in St. Louis in May 1805, the specimens were sent by boat to New Orleans, then on to Washington by way of Baltimore. They finally arrived in August. Jefferson was at Monticello, so he didn't get to look things over until early September. He then sent them to the American Philosophical Society in Philadelphia. He instructed the society to give the dried specimens to Dr. Benjamin Smith Barton, who was supposed to examine the collection and make a report.

This specimen of the leaves and flowers of the long-leaved sage collected by Lewis was sent to Jefferson on the keelboat in the spring of 1805.

When the explorers returned in 1806 with more specimens, Lewis traveled to Philadelphia to work out the details of how his plant collections would be handled. Dr. Barton was in poor health, so Lewis turned all his specimens over to the talented young botanist Frederick Pursh, who had worked for Barton. Then Lewis returned to St. Louis to take on his new job as the first governor of the Louisiana Territory.

Pursh worked hard at describing and drawing Lewis's plants. By May 1808 he had gone as far as he could without advice from Lewis, but Lewis didn't return to Philadelphia to help out. Pursh finally gave up on Lewis and headed for a new job in New York in the spring of 1809, taking a number of Lewis's specimens with him, as well as his drawings and descriptions.

Meriwether Lewis died on October 11, 1809, so the job of getting the journals and scientific information published fell to William Clark. Clark traveled to Philadelphia in January 1810 and saw the plant collection but didn't notice that some of the specimens were missing. We don't know what happened between Clark and Pursh. Pursh said later that he gave his drawings to Clark, but Clark never verified this, and we don't know if Clark paid Pursh more money for the work he'd done since Lewis had last paid him in 1807. Once again, Barton agreed to work on the plants, but once again he failed to come through, probably because of his ill health.

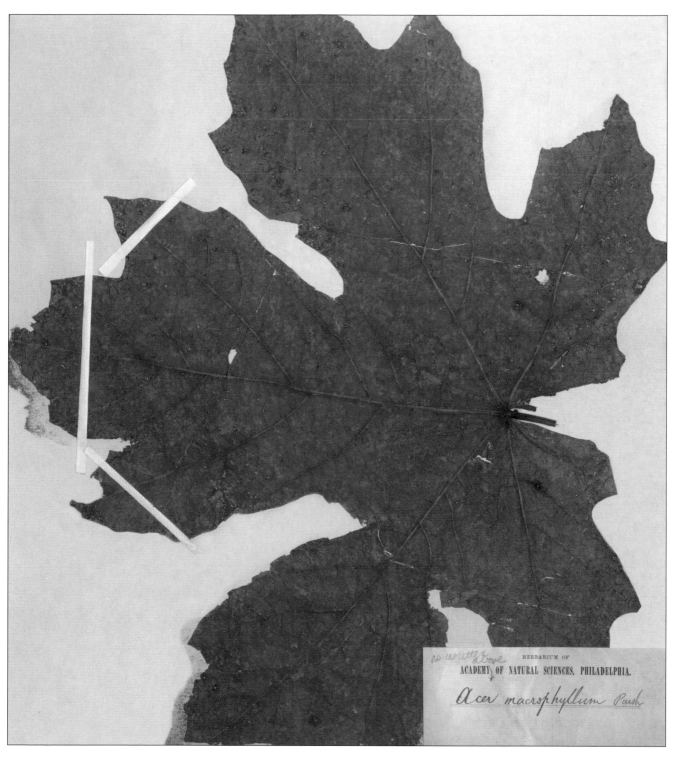

HERBARIUM OF
ACADEMY OF NATURAL SCIENCES, PHILADELPHIA.

as with above

Acer macrophyllum Pursh

Among the specimens preserved by Lewis that went to London with Pursh was this sample of a big-leaf maple. Its leaves are eight inches long and twelve inches wide. LEWIS AND CLARK HERBARIUM, AMERICAN PHILOSOPHICAL SOCIETY. PHOTO COURTESY OF THE ACADEMY OF NATURAL SCIENCES, PHILADELPHIA.

Pursh painted two different species of Fritillaria *that Lewis described.*

You can see from this photo of one Fritillaria, *called the yellow bell, how accurate Pursh's paintings are.*

Pursh went to London, where he devoted himself to writing the work that would make him famous: two beautifully illustrated volumes on the plants of America. In them he described 124 of the plants collected by Lewis and made more illustrations of them. He gave Lewis credit for the valuable information he had gathered. Besides honoring the explorers by using Lewis's name for the genus name of the bitterroot and Clark's for the ragged robin, he named three other species after Lewis: Lewis's syringa *(Philadelphus lewisii)*, often called the mock orange, which is now the state flower of Idaho; Lewis's wild flax *(Linum lewisii)*; and Lewis's monkey flower *(Mimulus lewisii)*. Thirteen of the twenty-seven illustrations he drew and painted of American wildflowers were of plants from the Lewis and Clark collection.

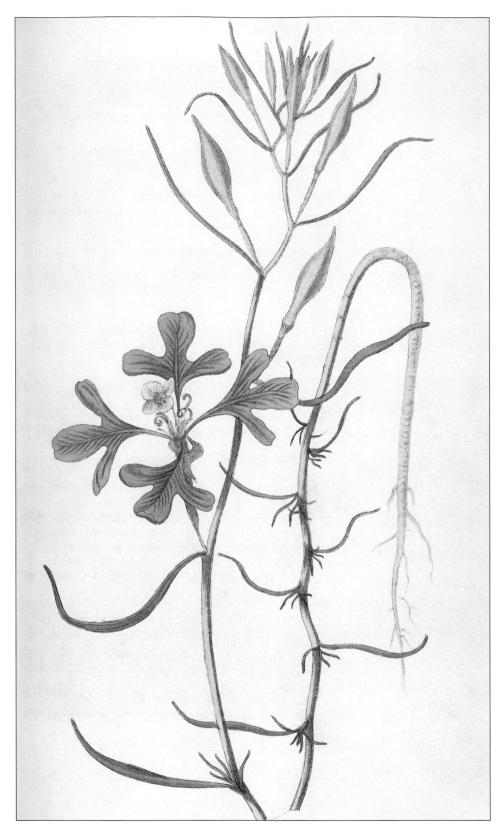

Here is Pursh's painting of Clarkia pulchella, *the plant he named after William Clark.* AMERICAN PHILOSOPHICAL SOCIETY

Tab. 20. p. 427.

Mimulus Lewisii.

Drawn & Engraved

The specimen Pursh used to paint Lewis's monkey flower has unfortunately disappeared.

By a stroke of luck, most of the specimens Pursh had taken with him eventually found their way back to Philadelphia. In 1842, after the deaths of Pursh and of his patron, A. B. Lambert, the plants were offered at auction in London. A young American botanist named Edward Tuckerman happened to attend the auction and bought the specimens. When he returned to the United States, he donated them to the Academy of Natural Sciences in Philadelphia. But not all of Pursh's specimens were in the auction lot, including Lewis's monkey flower. No one knows what happened to it.

In addition to scientific specimens, Lewis collected seeds, roots, and cuttings of plants. Some were shipped from the Mandan villages along with the plant specimens in 1805, and others came back with the expedition when it returned to St. Louis in 1806. A number of people were eager to grow these previously unknown plants in their gardens. Lewis and Clark both sent some seeds to relatives and friends, but we don't know what they did with them.

Three men with scientific interest were also given the chance to grow some of the new western plants: Thomas Jefferson; William Hamilton, a prominent botanist of the time; and Bernard McMahon, a well-known Philadelphia florist, gardener, and seed seller and the author of a 668-page botany reference book.

Jefferson grew corn from the Arikara and Mandan Indians. Ever the curious scientist, he compared it with corn sent to him from France. The Indian corn was of special interest because it was grown far to the north, where the growing season is short. He referred to one type as "quarantine corn." The original meaning of the word "quarantine" was a period of forty days. In Jefferson's garden, seeds planted on May 1 produced roasting ears by the last week of June, about eight weeks. A tenant gardener of Jefferson planted the same corn in the second week of May, and it was also ready to roast by the end of June—not much more than forty days after planting. The usual corn grown in those days took all summer to produce edible ears. Jefferson continued to grow the Indian varieties for several years. He also grew other plants from the expedition's seeds, including Arikara beans.

Willliam Hamilton didn't have much luck with Lewis's material. He wrote to Jefferson in February 1810: "Mr. Lewis's seeds have not yet vegetated [grown] freely, more however may come up with this coming spring. I have nevertheless obtained plants of the yellow wood, or Osage apple, seven or eight gooseberries, & one of his kinds of Arikara tobacco."

McMahon sent regular reports to Jefferson. We know that he was able to grow seven different species of currants, two of gooseberries, Indian tobacco, perennial flax, a species of huckleberry from Oregon, and a flowering pea. Thanks in part to McMahon, the snowberry, which has large white berries that

Snowberries, with their waxy white berries, add a nice touch to winter gardens.

stay on the plant all winter, and the dwarf juniper became familiar in American gardens.

McMahon also grew the Osage orange. Specimens believed to have originated from cuttings or seeds that Lewis sent to Jefferson still grow in the cemetery of St. Peter's Church, Philadelphia, which was once McMahon's garden.

Some of Lewis's plants crossed the Atlantic to Europe, including the snowberry, and seed catalogs in America advertised some of the plants. In 1815 "The American Gardener's Almanac" offered for sale seeds of Mandan corn, Arikara beans, perennial flax, and the snowberry. Many of these plants have disappeared from American gardens, but a few are still grown today, including several kinds of currant, the Osage orange, and the Oregon grape.

For a number of reasons, Lewis's accomplishments as a naturalist were largely ignored for more than 150 years. When the first version of the journals finally came out in 1814, little of the information on animals and plants was included in the narrative, which had been edited by a young lawyer named Nicolas Biddle. Benjamin Smith Barton was supposed to produce the volume on the natural history, but he never did. For many years most people were unaware of the scientific work accomplished on the expedition.

Almost eighty years later, in 1893, naturalist Elliott Coues

The Oregon grape is grown as an ornamental plant in home gardens today.

reissued Biddle's work and added many footnotes, including some on the plants and animals. This was followed by a much-expanded version published on the hundredth anniversary of the journey in 1904. Even so, the natural history still took a back seat to other aspects of the expedition.

Finally, in 1969 *Lewis and Clark: Pioneering Naturalists* by Paul Russell Cutright was published. Cutright went through the original journals laboriously and traveled fifteen thousand miles over a period of several years to complete his research. He visited every museum and library he could find that had specimens or information relating to the expedition, and he conferred with scientists and scholars across the country. Cutright also followed the trail from beginning to end, dividing his own journey of discovery into six trips.

Cutright listed the plants that Lewis had noted for science for the first time. He also sorted through the various collections

When the Corps of Discovery passed through the Bitterroot Valley, much of the land away from the shore of the river was infested with prickly pear cactus. The climate there is naturally quite dry.

Today, the Bitterroot Valley is lush and green from irrigated pastures and fields of crops.

in the Academy of Natural Sciences in Philadelphia for specimens from the expedition and persuaded the academy to keep all the Lewis and Clark specimens together in one collection.

From the mid-1980s through the 1990s, Gary E. Moulton of the University of Nebraska devoted his energies to editing all the known journals from the Lewis and Clark expedition, including those written by other members. Every word they

The wakerobin is another plant Lewis described for science for the first time.

wrote is now available to readers and researchers. Moulton's volumes are peppered with informative footnotes as well, many of which identify or add information about the plants the explorers encountered along the way. In this book, Moulton's names for the plants are used. When a plant's modern name isn't in his volumes, Cutright's terms are used.

Thanks to Cutright and Moulton, we now realize what the most important accomplishments of the Lewis and Clark expedition were. Thanks to these remarkable explorers, we have vital information not only about the plants but also about the geology, geography, and animals of western North America before its settlement by European Americans. We can look back in time and see the landscapes before they became crisscrossed by railroads and freeways, blanketed by farms and ranches, and dotted by the cities and towns of the present-day United States.

To Learn More

I relied on many sources for information in writing this book, including Stephen Ambrose's fine biography of Meriwether Lewis, *Undaunted Courage* (New York: Simon & Schuster, 1996). Paul Russell Cutright chronicles the plants, animals, and Indians in *Lewis & Clark: Pioneering Naturalists* (Lincoln, Nebraska: University of Nebraska Press, 1989). *Lewis and Clark Among the Indians* by James P. Ronda (Lincoln, Nebraska: University of Nebraska Press, 1989) tells of the explorers' interactions with the Indians. Daniel B. Botkin uses the Lewis and Clark expedition as a way of looking at conservation issues today in *Our Natural History: The Lessons of Lewis and Clark* (New York: G.P. Putnam's Sons, 1995).

The complete journals have been faithfully transcribed from the originals and edited by Gary E. Moulton, who also provides extensive notes in *The Journals of the Lewis & Clark Expedition, Volumes 1 to 13* (Lincoln, Nebraska: University of Nebraska Press, 1987-2001). *The Journals of Lewis and Clark*, edited by Bernard De Voto (New York: Mariner Books, 1997), is an excellent selection of journal entries.

Many guide books are available for families who want to explore the Lewis and Clark Trail, which has been designated a National Historic Trail. Museums and other sites along the route have exhibits filled with artifacts and fascinating information. *Plants of the Lewis and Clark Expedition,* by H. Wayne Phillips (Missoula, Montana: Mountain Press, 2003) has information about and photos of every plant Lewis collected. *Along the Trail with Lewis and Clark,* second edition (Helena, Montana: Montana Magazine/Farcountry Press, 2002) by Barbara Fifer and Vicky Soderberg has lots of quotations from the journals and excellent maps prepared by Joseph Mussulman, as well as abundant information about sites along the way. *Backtracking by Foot, Canoe, and Subaru Along the Lewis and Clark Trail* (Seattle, Washington: Sasquatch Books, 2000) by Benjamin Long is an interesting modern-day adventure, with information about some of the plants and animals mentioned in the journals.

William Muñoz and I have collaborated on two other books about Lewis and Clark: *Animals on the Trail with Lewis and Clark* (New York: Clarion Books, 2002), which describes the animals they found, including information on how the animals lived before European American settlement, and *The Lewis and Clark Trail Then and Now* (New York: Dutton Children's Books, 2002), which tells of the differences in life and landscape between 1804–1806 and today. *The Incredible Journey of*

Lewis and Clark by Rhoda Blumberg (Magnolia, Massachusetts: Peter Smith Publishers, 1999), is an award-winning book for young people that gives an overall view of the expedition.

For those who explore the Internet, "Lewis & Clark on the Information Superhighway" *(http://www.lcarchive.org/fulllist.html)* provides links to every site on the web that concerns Lewis and Clark. A couple of especially good sites are "Discovering Lewis and Clark" *(http://www.lewis-clark.org)* and the official home of the Lewis and Clark Trail Heritage Foundation, Inc. *(http://www.lewisandclark.org)*. I also have information about my own experiences along the trail on my website, *http://www.dorothyhinshawpatent.com*.

Plant Specimens in the Lewis and Clark Herbarium

*P*lants mentioned in the journals but not surviving as specimens do not appear in the following list, so some of the plants discussed in the text are absent. Specimens of 177 different plant species represented by 239 specimens survive in the Lewis and Clark Herbarium. Most of these—227 specimens—are at the Academy of Natural Sciences in Philadelphia. Kew Gardens in England has eleven specimens. One problematical specimen, the snowberry, is at the Charleston Museum in Charleston, South Carolina, and may have been preserved later, from a plant grown from seeds provided by Lewis. Some species were already known to science, but Lewis's observations extended their known range. Most, however, were species new to science at the time Lewis collected them. I have based this list on Gary E. Moulton's "Table of the Herbarium by Date Collected" in *The Journals of the Lewis & Clark Expedition, Volume 12: Herbarium of the Lewis & Clark Expedition*. Each plant is listed only once, the first time it was collected.

1804

Up the Missouri River

August 10	Field horsetail	Burt County, Nebraska or Monona County, Iowa
August 17	Meadow anemone	Dakota County, Nebraska
August 17	Curly-top gumweed	Dakota County, Nebraska
August 25	Rocky Mountain bee plant	Clay County, South Dakota, or Cedar or Dixon County, Nebraska
September 1	Wild four-o'clock	Bon Homme County, South Dakota, or Knox County, Nebraska
September 2	Pasture sagewort	Bon Homme County, South Dakota, or Knox County, Nebraska
September 2	Purple prairie clover	Bon Homme County, South Dakota, or Knox County, Nebraska
September 4	Buffaloberry	Knox County, Nebraska, or Bon Homme County, South Dakota
September 5	Bur oak	Knox County, Nebraska, or Charles Mix County, South Dakota
September 5	Prairie wild rose	Knox County, Nebraska, or Charles Mix County, South Dakota
September 8	Wild rice	Charles Mix or Gregory County, South Dakota, or Boyd County, Nebraska
September 12	Gay-feather	Brule County, South Dakota
September 15	Silky wormwood	Lyman or Brule County, South Dakota
September 15	Canada milk-vetch	Lyman or Brule County, South Dakota
September 15	Spiny goldenweed	Lyman or Brule County, South Dakota
September 18	Missouri milk-vetch	Lyman or Brule County, South Dakota

September 18	Blazing star	Lyman or Brule County, South Dakota
September 19	Snakeweed	Big Bend of the Missouri River, South Dakota
September 21	Aromatic aster	Big Bend of the Missouri River
September 21	Four-wing saltbush	Big Bend of the Missouri River
September 21	Wild alfalfa	Big Bend of the Missouri River
September 21	Lance-leaved sage	Big Bend of the Missouri River
September 21	Rabbit brush	Big Bend of the Missouri River
October 1	Fragrant sumac	Dewey, Sully, or Stanley County, South Dakota
October 1	Dwarf sagebrush	Dewey, Sully, or Stanley County, South Dakota
October 1	White sage	Dewey, Sully, or Stanley County, South Dakota
October 2	Rocky Mountain juniper	Dewey or Sully County, South Dakota
October 3	Long-leaved sage	Potter-Sully county line, South Dakota
October 4	Fire-on-the-mountain	Dewey or Potter County, South Dakota
October 12	Indian tobacco	Campbell or Corson County, South Dakota
October 16	Creeping juniper	Sioux or Emmons County, North Dakota
October 16	Silver-leaf scurf-pea	Sioux or Emmons County, North Dakota
October 17	Common juniper	Sioux or Emmons County, North Dakota
Winter '04–'05	Bearberry	Fort Mandan, McLean County, North Dakota

1805

Montana and Idaho

July 29	Golden currant	Three Forks of the Missouri River, Montana
September 2	Trumpet honeysuckle	North Fork of the Salmon River, Idaho
September 2	Mountain ash	North Fork of the Salmon River, Idaho
September 3	Angelica?	Lost Trail Pass, Montana/Idaho border
October 1	Ponderosa pine	Canoe camp, Clearwater County, Idaho

Washington and Oregon

October ?	Oregon white-topped aster	Snake River, Washington
October ?	Calliopsis	Snake River, Washington
October 31?	Vine maple	Cascades of the Columbia River, Washington/Oregon border
October 31?	Dull Oregon grape	Cascades of the Columbia River, Washington/Oregon border
October ?	Hoary aster	Columbia River
November 1	Pacific madrone	Cascades of the Columbia River, Washington/Oregon border
November 16	Mountain-box	Pacific County, Washington
November 17	Menzies' rockweed	Pacific County, Washington

1806

January 20	Deer fern	Fort Clatsop, Oregon
January 20	Mountain wood-fern	Fort Clatsop, Oregon
January 20	Salal	Fort Clatsop, Oregon

January 20	Moss species	Fort Clatsop, Oregon
January 20	Dwarf bilberry	Fort Clatsop, Oregon
January 27	Evergreen huckleberry	Fort Clatsop, Oregon
March 13	Silverweed	Fort Clatsop, Oregon
March 13	Edible thistle	Fort Clatsop, Oregon
March 13	Foxtail barley	Fort Clatsop, Oregon

HOMEWARD BOUND

March 26	Red alder	Cowlitz County, Washington, or Columbia County, Oregon
March 26	Littleleaf montia	Cowlitz County, Washington, or Columbia County, Oregon
March 26	Garry oak	Cowlitz County, Washington, or Columbia County, Oregon
March 27	Red currant	Cowlitz County, Washington, or Columbia County, Oregon
March 27	Salmonberry	Cowlitz County, Washington, or Columbia County, Oregon
April 1	Slender toothwort	Sandy River, Oregon
April 8	Siberian montia	Mulnomah County, Oregon, or Skamania County, Washington
April 8	Straggly gooseberry	Mulnomah County, Oregon, or Skamania County, Washington
April 10	Checker lily	Bradford Island, Oregon
April 10	Big-leaf maple	Cascades of the Columbia River, Washington/Oregon border
April 10	White trillium	Cascades of the Columbia River, Washington/Oregon border
April 11	Oregon grape	Cascades of the Columbia River, Washington/Oregon border

April 14	Menzies' larkspur	Skamania or Klickitat County, Washington, or Hood River or Wasco County, Oregon
April 14	Lomatium	Klickitat County, Washington, or Wasco County, Oregon
April 14	Lomatium (different species?)	Skamania or Klickitat County, Washington, or Hood River or Wasco County, Oregon
April 14	Arrowleaf balsamroot	Skamania or Klickitat County, Washington, or Hood River or Wasco County, Oregon
April 15	Serviceberry	The Dalles of the Columbia River, Washington/Oregon border
April 15	Barestem lomatium	The Dalles of the Columbia River, Washington/Oregon border
April 15	Lomatium species	The Dalles of the Columbia River, Washington/Oregon border
April 15	Thimbleberry	The Dalles of the Columbia River, Washington/Oregon border
April 16	Jeffrey's shooting star	The Dalles of the Columbia River, Washington/Oregon border
April 17	Ranchers fiddleneck	Rock Fort Camp, Oregon
April 17	Miner's lettuce	Rock Fort Camp, Oregon
April 17	Small-flowered blue-eyed Mary	Rock Fort Camp, Oregon
April 17	Narrow-leaf collomia	Rock Fort Camp, Oregon
April 17	Lindley's microseris	Rock Fort Camp, Oregon
April 17	Threadleaf phacelia	Rock Fort Camp, Oregon
April 17	Slender plagiobothrys	Rock Fort Camp, Oregon
April 17	Big-head clover	Rock Fort Camp, Oregon
April 20	Douglas' brodiaea	The Dalles of the Columbia River

April 22	Field chickweed	Klickitat County, Washington, or Wasco or Sherman County, Oregon
April 25	Western sweet-cicely	Klickitat or Benton County, Washington, or Gilliam or Morrow County, Oregon
April 29	Black hawthorn	Walla Walla River, Washington
April 29	Cous	Walla Walla River, Washington
April 30	Textile onion	Walla Walla River, Washington

IDAHO

May 6	Green rabbit brush	Clearwater River
May 6	Nine-leaf lomatium	Clearwater River
May 6	Lewis's syringa	Clearwater River
May 7	Showy phlox	Nez Perce County
May 8	Yellow bell	Clearwater River
May 8	Pale fawn-lily	Clearwater River
May 17	Northwest mariposa	Camp Chopunnish
May 20	Yarrow	Camp Chopunnish
May 20	Wilcox's penstemon	Camp Chopunnish
May 27	Douglas's clematis	Camp Chopunnish
May 29	Cascara	Camp Chopunnish
May 29	Creambush ocean-spray	Camp Chopunnish
May 29	Bitter cherry	Camp Chopunnish
May 29	Chokecherry	Camp Chopunnish
June 1	Ragged robin	Camp Chopunnish
June 1	Rough wallflower	Camp Chopunnish
June 5	Narrow-leaved skullcap	Camp Chopunnish
June 5	Wormleaf stonecrop	Camp Chopunnish
June 5	Silky lupine	Camp Chopunnish

June 6	Common eriophyllum	Camp Chopunnish
June 9	Varileaf phacelia	Camp Chopunnish
June 10	Idaho fescue	Camp Chopunnish
June 10	Prairie Junegrass	Camp Chopunnish
June 10	Fern-leaved lomatium	Camp Chopunnish
June 10	Sandberg's bluegrass	Camp Chopunnish
June 10	Bluebunch wheatgrass	Camp Chopunnish
June 12	Old man's whiskers	Weippe Prairie
June 12	Pineapple weed	Weippe Prairie
June 12	American bistort	Weippe Prairie
June 14	Long-leaf evening primrose	Weippe Prairie
June 14	Clustered frasera	Weippe Prairie
June 15	Wood anemone	Lolo Trail
June 15	Shrubby penstemon	Lolo Trail
June 15	Purple trillium	Lolo Trail
June 15	Indian basket-grass	Lolo Trail
June 16	Fairy-slipper	Lolo Trail
June 16	Bunchberry	Lolo Trail
June 16	Sticky currant	Lolo Trail
June 23	Camas	Weippe Prairie
June 25	California false hellebore	Lolo Trail
June 26	Scarlet gilia	Lolo Trail
June 26	Mountain kittentails	Lolo Trail
June 27	Redstem ceanothus	Lolo Trail
June 27	Western springbeauty	Lolo Trail
June 27	Threeleaved lewisia	Lolo Trail
June 27	Western polemonium	Lolo Trail
June ?	Black cottonwood	unknown

MONTANA

July 1	Liverwort species	Travelers' Rest
July 1	Bitterroot	Travelers' Rest
July 1	Thin-leaved owl-clover	Travelers' Rest
July 1	Small-head clover	Travelers' Rest
July 1?	Bessey's crazyweed	Travelers' Rest
July 4	Yellow monkey-flower	Blackfoot River
July 5	Western blue flag	Nevada Valley
July 6	Silverberry	Nevada Valley
July 6	Fern-leaved lousewort	Blackfoot River
July 6	Pink elephants	Blackfoot River
July 6	Shrubby cinquefoil	Nevada Valley
July 6	Antelope-brush	Nevada Valley
July 7	Blanket flower	Lewis and Clark Pass
July 7	Bearberry honeysuckle	Lewis and Clark Pass
July 7	White camas	Blackfoot River
July 7	Silvery lupine	Blackfoot River
July 8	Needle-and-thread	Lewis and Clark or Teton County
July 9	Blue flax	Lewis and Clark, Teton, or Cascade County
July 17	Gumbo evening primrose	Great Falls of the Missouri River
July 20	Moundscale	Marias River
July 20	Greasewood	Marias River
July 20	Red false mallow	Marias River
July 28	Snow-on-the-mountain	Rosebud County

FINAL STRETCH

August 10	White milkwort	Williams or McKenzie County, North Dakota
August 27	False indigo	Big Bend of the Missouri River, South Dakota
August ?	Cottonwood	unknown
September 8	Raccoon grape	Council Bluff, Nebraska
September 12	Rigid goldenrod	Doniphan or Atchison County, Kansas, or Buchanan County, Missouri
unknown	Rusty lupine	Missouri River?
unknown	Indian breadroot	Missouri River?
unknown	Lemon scurf-pea	Missouri River?
unknown	Snowberry	Missouri River?
unknown	Mountain balm	Clearwater River, Idaho
unknown	Cut-leaved daisy	Clearwater River, Idaho
unknown	Dune wildrye	unknown
unknown	Osage orange	unknown
unknown	Clammy-weed	unknown

Index

Page numbers in **bold** type refer to illustrations.